THE THINGS OF GOD

Reverend James E. Harrell Jr.

To order additional copies of this book, contact:

Xlibris
844-714-8691
www.Xlibris.com
Orders@Xlibris.com

ISBN: Softcover   978-1-6698-6434-9
        EBook   978-1-6698-6433-2

Print information available on the last page

Rev. date: 01/31/2023

¹² And I turned to see the voice that spake with me. And being turned, I saw seven gold candlesticks;

¹³ And in the midst of the seven candlesticks *one* like unto the Son of man, clothed with garment down to the foot, and girt about the paps with a golden girdle.

¹⁴ His head and *his* hairs *were* white like wool, as white as snow; and his eyes *were* as a flar of fire;

¹⁵ And his feet like unto fine brass, as if they burned in a furnace; and his voice as the sou of many waters.

¹⁶ And he had in his right hand seven stars: and out of his mouth went a sharp twoedg sword: and his countenance *was* as the sun shineth in his strength.

¹⁷ And when I saw him, I fell at his feet as dead. And he laid his right hand upon me, sayi

Pastor James E. Harrell Jr., thank God for my family and their influences in my life. I thank im for those whom He allows in the path of my life. How could any man say that he is o od when he does not love God's creation? The answer is that he is not of God, nor now o ver would be. Some things are plain sight and obvious. How could a man claim to be saved nd refuse to love a man because of the color of his skin? The answer is that he is not saved od is love and loved the whole world that He gave Jesus to live and die so we could be with im. How could you serve a savior that you hate? The answer is that you deceive yourself.

he intent of my book is to bring us into the reality of knowing and understanding the things at are of God. To do this is to accept what is true and to reject the father of lies, who is atan. What is true is the Triune God. You cannot accept what you do not receive. Those tha ve can enter by the blood of Jesus Christ, the Son of God.

John 2:18-19 (KJV)

Little children, it is the last time: and as ye have heard that antichrist shall come, even now re there many antichrists; whereby we know that it is the last time.

They went out from us, but they were not of us; for if they had been of us, they would no oubt have continued with us: but they went out, that they might be made manifest that they ere not all of us.

CHAPTER ONE

Genesis Seven Days of Creation

Readers do read: Genesis 1: 1-31 and 2: 1-3

God had created the angels, animals, mammals, and men, just as God created the heavens hosts, and the Earth in the beginning. God is supreme, and God is divine, and God is infinite in all that He is and in all that He does. God is omnipotent, all-powerful. We cannot describe God's greatness in the very essence that He is. Even an eternity with God is not long enough to know everything God is. 1 Corinthians 2:10-11 (KJV) "But God hath revealed *them* unto us by his Spirit: for the Spirit searcheth all things, yea, the deep things of God. For what man knoweth the things of a man, save the spirit of man which is in him? even so the things of God knoweth no man, but the Spirit of God." Therefore, God will be just in His judgment of humankind. The Spirit of God bears witness with the spirit of men (Romans 8:16), and our heart does not lie to the Spirit of Truth.

God, who is Jesus, says that the disobedience worships Him with their mouths and honor with their lips and not with their heart in Isaiah 29:13 and Matthew 15:8. The Bible also teaches us that we must worship God in truth and spirit in John 4:24. And our treasures are in the same place of the heart (Matthew 6:21). To God be the glory for He is all-knowing, omniscient and is omnipresent, meaning everywhere. To name one of the major differences between God and man is that God knows who He is, but you and I take God to reveal who we indeed are so that we may know ourselves.

At the beginning of Genesis 1:1, the earth was without form, void, and darkness was on the face of the deep. The Hebrew Bible said that when God created heaven and earth, the earth welter, waste, and night over the deep. Likewise, angels and men are nothing short of void, empty, and dark without God. The Word of God says that "the imagination of man's heart is evil from his youth" (Genesis 8:21), but God put the remedy for sin in place because of a soothing aroma. There is nothing of any hope without God. But because God exists, there are order, decency, and creations.

Also, the Bible says that the Spirit of God was hovering over the face of the waters. God's very breath was hovering over the waters. Have you ever breathed over a bowl or a cup of water and felt the air bounce off the water back onto your face? The same breath God blows into Adam's nostrils is imitated in all nostrils. The very essence of life is in the blood, but the breath of God jump-starts life.

The next thing God did was say, "let there be light," and He saw it, and it was. God sent Jesus into the world to be The Beacon of Light, but the prophets, judges, priests, John the Baptist, the Apostles, and us, the disciples of Jesus, are the beacon of the Light of Beacon, Jesus Christ. John was the one who prepared the way for his cousin, Emmanuel, Jesus. I think of two things; the parable of the wheat and tares; Jesus teaches, "The kingdom of heaven is like a man who sowed good seed in his field; but while men slept, his enemy came and sowed tares among the wheat and went his way (Matthews 13). Secondly, when God was not in the Garden of Eden, Satan had found a way to corrupt Adam, but like the owner of the field, when the servants came to him to tell him that weeds came up with the grain that produced a crop, and he said let it be. God uses that which is counted against us to be good for us. Only God could make crooked straight.

"Likewise, when Noah had built an altar unto God and put upon it clean animals and clean birds, God smelled a sweet savor and said in His heart, I will not again curse the ground anymore for man's sake" (Genesis 8:20-21). It was then, God who knows all, had decided to let the good and the bad survive together. But it was back when God saw Noah as a grain that came up in the field; He decided to spare humanity. And God said that the light was good. And God divided the light from the darkness, calling the light day and the darkness night. So then, we being in darkness, have the light of good in us.

Good and evil in us start in our minds and hearts. Your decision sinks into the heart. Adam's thought process went from Adam's mind to his very nature, his heart. Adam and Eve had to tell God why they hid from Him because the enemy had come in the night. So, God had to reveal to man his sins. He did this through Moses with the Ten Commandments, yet Adam already knew they had sinned.

God separated the light from the darkness by making it known who we are apart from Him. God called the light day and the darkness; He called night. The day was not daytime, and the night was not nighttime on this day. Simply light was called day, and darkness was called night. John 1:5 (CSBBible) reads, "That light shines in the darkness, and yet the darkness did not overcome it." A house with multiple rooms with no light is dark. (Remember, the light here is called day, rather it be a candle, lamp, flashlight, etc.) When light is in any room lights, there is the day in that room, but the other rooms remain dark. God lighted a lamp (called the light day) to reveal the face of the Earth. Still, there was darkness everywhere else (a dark closet, dark tunnel, dark secret, etc., because of darkness, it is called night). God makes the invisible things visible (spiritual warfare) so that we may know a God of creation exists. And many remain in darkness, and they shall be without excuses.

Move out of the darkness and come into the light.

Without God, there is no light. God gave us hope for salvation. An excellent thing to be able to see the light. And the evening and the morning were day one. Like the field owner who said separation would happen at harvest time. The harvest occurred in the 1st Resurrection, not the 2nd Resurrection. John said that he saw the dead (the 2nd Resurrection) standing before God and the books, and another book, the book of life, opened (Revelation 20:12). The saved in Christ had already been harvested. Amen.

On day two, Genesis 1:6, God separates the waters by making a firmament. There were now waters above the firmament and waters beneath the firmament. The firmament is called Heaven. The Hebrew Bible calls heaven the vault, meaning Heavens (1st, 2nd, and 3rd Heaven), the sky, outer space, and the Kingdom of Heaven. So, God determines what is on each side of heaven about the Earth's waters. But God is not finished with the waters.

On day three, Genesis 1:9, the waters under the heavens gathered in one place, and the land appeared before God. Now, remember birds of a feather flock together. There was one piece of land before it had divided as the world is today. Now the ground is called Earth, but the waters are called Seas. The earth's land had in it various seeds that grow and replicate themselves.

And pertaining to the new world to come will not have Seas (Revelation 21:1). Today, there is a place where the salt and fresh waters touch but do not mix, called "estuaries/brackish." These two water bodies that join without mixing alone vividly show God's awesomeness. But when we read about it in the Bible, seas always represent trouble. In Christ, we are walking on solid ground, and our problems count as joy. In Christ, there is good seeding. Without God, there is no peace but always trouble. Jesus can calm any storm you encounter, just as He did in the boat over the stormy sea.

On day four, Genesis 1:14, God said let there be lights in the firmament of the heavens to divide the day from the night. The manifestation had taken place in the heavens first. Manifestation occurs first in the spiritual realm and then in the physical realm. After all, God is Spirit and created all things. God then said for the lights in the firmament of the heavens to give light to the Earth, for its signs, seasons, days, and years. God foreknew even our spirits before the foundation of the world (Ephesians 1:4) because spiritual matters take place first in heaven. The foundation is the very core of the Earth before the Earth was without form, void, and darkness was on the face of the deep.

On the fourth day, we see God's command to the light in the sky. The day and the night are equal in mass, but the light from the sky ruled where the day was, and the night was. Imagine all the lights in the house are off. The whole house now has light because of the light in the firmament and not just in one or two rooms. In this world, there is a balance of right and wrong ways. Where we see good, there is also evil to ward off. But looking to God, He is the focus for godliness. God is the light in the sky of our lives.

Then He makes two great lights and sets them in the firmament of the heavens to also give light on the Earth: the more excellent light to rule the day and the lesser light to rule the night with the help of the stars. Sometimes you could look up at the sky and see the moon while the sun is out, but you never could see the sun while the moon is out at night. The sun is like the pastor of the church. It could see the bigger vision.

The congregation, with multiple insights into the bigger vision, is like the moon, with the sun as the under-shepherd. Unlike the two great lights on the cloudiest day, the lights in the firmament of the heavens will always obey its decree and give light to the Earth. Even when it is daytime, we don't always see the sunshine. So, when your sun does not shine, know that God is still able. Without God, there is no order. Therefore, those in Christ can rejoice with God no matter how dark their day may be.

On day five, Genesis 1:20, God spoke and said let the waters abound with an abundance of living creatures, and let birds fly above the Earth across the face of the firmament of the heavens. We will address whom God chooses to consult with before creating matters, yet God is God alone. Then God, after consulting, had made great sea creatures and every living thing that moves, with which the waters abounded, according to their kind, and every winged bird according to its kind. God then commissioned them to be fruitful and multiply. Wise men seek counseling when it comes to essential matters. They do their research, and they study their research. Now I am talking about wise men and not a scientist, a politician, a royal people (Christians are royal people), but unless they are savvy as individuals in God's way, then know that I am speaking about wise men, women, boys, or girls. Also, rhetorically speaking, have you ever seen a male dog make love to a male dog? God told everything in the sea to fill the sea by being fruitful and multiply and of the air likewise. Amen. Without God, there is no self-preservation. And where there is no self-preservation, there is no wisdom to the wise and those who believe they are brilliant.

On day six, Genesis 1:24, God consulted again and said the "let" word again "Let the earth bring forth the living creature according to its kind: cattle and creeping thing and beast of the earth, each according to its kind." We see and understand that the word "let" in God's speaking is to suggest what He is going to do, something miraculous, and then the word says, "and it was so," meaning being in one accord and to fully agree.

Then God made every form of animal and creeping thing, putting them on the Earth. God teaches us through the book of John 1:1-3 (KJV), "In the beginning was the Word, and the Word was with God, and the Word was God. The same was in the beginning with God. All things were made by him; and without him was not any thing made that was made", and through the book of John 1:14 (KJV), God teaches us, "And the Word was made flesh, and dwelt among us, (and we beheld his glory, the glory as of the only begotten of the Father,) full of grace and truth."

But also, on day six, Genesis 1:26-27, God said, "let us make man in Our image, according to Our likeness: and let them have dominion over the fish to the sea, over the birds of the air, and over the cattle, over all the earth and over every creeping thing that creeps on the earth." Here God consulted twice, once for making man and once for giving them dominion. But always the consultation first, and then God would act. But what does not follow this time like in day five is "and it was so," because there was a disagreement. God when He said, "let us" He was consulting not for their permission but informing the angels what He was about to do, but God believes in unity, one accord, decency and orderly. God does nothing without letting the faithful know, and He calls us friends.

Guess who disagreed with God wanting to create man in their image when God said, "let us make man in our image and in our likeness." That's right; Satan and the 1/3 angels followed him and fell from heaven. Then "God created man in His own image in the image of God, He created him; male and female He created them." (Ezekiel 8:2 CSBBible) "I looked, and there was someone who looked like a man. From what seemed to be his waist down was fire, and from his waist up was something that looked bright, like the gleam of amber.").

God is Omnipotent, and God is God. God doesn't need our permission to do anything. God is Omniscient and makes ways out of no ways. So, God did not create man in the image of them all, as He had consulted to do but instead, He made man in His own image, **but** in what manner? Psalm 8:4-9 (KJV) "What is man, that thou art mindful of him? and the son of man, that thou visitest him? For thou hast made him a little lower than the angels, and hast crowned him with glory and honour. Thou madest him to have dominion over the works of thy hands; thou hast put all *things* under his feet: All sheep and oxen, yea, and the beasts of the field; The fowl of the air, and the fish of the sea, *and whatsoever* passeth through the paths of the seas. O LORD our Lord, how excellent *is* thy name in all the Earth," which is that manner. Amen. And God even made himself in the image of man. We know Him as Jesus Christ, our Lord, and Savior in the flesh. But God never stops being God. God never leaves His throne. God never died as God the Creator. God never died as God the Father. God died as God the Son, but He rose on the third day. We call Jesus' death our atonement. We call Jesus' risen from the grave the "day of Resurrection".

Your sins and the sins of the world, Jesus Christ, a divine man, died for. Divine means being born of the virgin Mary, impregnated by the Holy Ghost, being without sin yet tempted with all wrong, and worthy of being God's Son. Jesus is God and the Son of God, and our spirit seeks after God's own image (bodily figure, our mind, and spirit). We must worship God in truth and spirit. Through repentance, we are without corruption. We are once again made whole and not broken anymore, in the image that men once were, in the image of God, and should be in the likeness of angels. Oh, it will be something to be in the image of God being not of the flesh, Philippians 3:21 (NIV) "who, by the power that enables him to bring everything under his control, will transform our lowly bodies so that they will be like his glorious body."

On day seven, Genesis 2:2, God rested. There is salvation in God through the blood of Jesus. By it, God promises that the gift of God is eternal life. In Matthew 11:28-30 (KJV), Jesus says, "Come unto me, all ye that labour and are heavy laden, and I will give you rest. Take my yoke upon you, and learn of me; for I am meek and lowly in heart: and ye shall find rest unto your souls. For my yoke *is* easy, and my burden is light."

CHAPTER TWO

Getting On Board

I start this chapter at the end and finish at the beginning because it is always at the start that preachers have your 100% attention. Somebody has been praying and will always be praying about their ministry. And because of that, I am starting by saying things from Proverbs. Proverbs 12:1 (HCSB) "Whoever loves discipline loves knowledge, but one who hates correction is stupid." Now that I got your full attention and in the name of Jesus Christ, our Lord and Savior, I apologize if I come across to you abruptly. I said, Lord, this is not an easy sermon, but God desires obedience over sacrifice. Amen.

Looking at Jesus' inner disciplining since age 12, we must understand that this had already developed in him before 12. The internal battle is between your flesh and your spirit. Before you can minister a ministry, you must first understand structure. Jesus knew the struggles within him, for he, too, was tempted in all ways, even as we are. Before starting your ministry, you must learn to look where God is already working. You cannot expect to begin an effective ministry when you cannot tune into what God is already doing and become a part of that. You learn to get on board when you know to seek and work where God is working. God's answers to your request become yea and Amen. Learning comes when you engage in God's will. It is not about your friends because it is about you and God. A personal relationship with God is experiencing God. You could do nothing new as a ministry, but God does change methods. God is the same all the time, but He does use different forms, and God already knows who belongs to Him. He will send you to those appointed to step in your path or send them to you. But the relationship could be for a moment, season, or long-term.

Your duty is to become holy as God is holy; this is your reasonable service. Learning how to wear the Full Armor of God, what it means to do things in decency and order, and how to be indwelled by the Holy Spirit and filled with the Holy Spirit. Running from place to place only makes you the LCM. God is disciplining you to be of the age of accountability. In Christ, you learn to conquer the battles within yourself before defeating them externally. Jesus understood disciplining and being about his Father's business. Amen.

Luke 2:41-52 (KJV)

[41] Now his parents went to Jerusalem every year at the feast of the Passover.

⁴² And when he was twelve years old, they went up to Jerusalem after the custom of the feast.

⁴³ And when they had fulfilled the days, as they returned, the child Jesus tarried behind in Jerusalem; and Joseph and his mother knew not *of it*.

⁴⁴ But they, supposing him to have been in the company, went a day's journey; and they sought him among *their* kinsfolk and acquaintance.

⁴⁵ And when they found him not, they turned back again to Jerusalem, seeking him.

⁴⁶ And it came to pass, that after three days they found him in the temple, sitting in the midst of the doctors, both hearing them, and asking them questions.

⁴⁷ And all that heard him were astonished at his understanding and answers.

⁴⁸ And when they saw him, they were amazed: and his mother said unto him, Son, why hast thou thus dealt with us? behold, thy father and I have sought thee sorrowing.

⁴⁹ And he said unto them, How is it that ye sought me? wist ye not that I must be about my Father's business?

⁵⁰ And they understood not the saying which he spake unto them.

⁵¹ And he went down with them, and came to Nazareth, and was subject unto them: but his mother kept all these sayings in her heart.

⁵² And Jesus increased in wisdom and stature, and in favour with God and man.

Jesus disciplined himself when he was old enough to understand His calling. That calling for me was when I was 31 years old. Jesus, he had been about his father's business at a young age. Jesus had already been in preparation for God in Heaven, his biological father's business. At 12, he held the attention of established men in the law. They knew doctorates and were masters of the Law of the things of God. Jesus carried himself in the like discipline of these much-educated men. As we read, Jesus continues to grow and earn favor with God and man. Jesus had already shown himself to be faithful in the attendance of the temple, trained into being reliable by God, our Heavenly Father.

Jesus was there for three days before Mary and Joseph caught up with him, and after they found Him, they still had not caught up with Him spiritually. Mary would hide things in her heart that Jesus said. Mary and Joseph knew how to hold the traditions of God and the Jews, but Mary and Joseph were not doctors in the temple. These doctors and whoever else heard Jesus were astonished at both Jesus' questions and Jesus' answers. Jesus was so disciplined that it was one day before his parents realized He was not with them. Whereas my parents would suspect me of mischief when I became quiet. However, Jesus was about His father's business and being in a safe place.

When I was of the world as a grown man, you would hear my name come up in many conversations because I was no angel. When I decided to live for Christ, the lesser my name would come up in worldly gossip, the more it would come up as spiritual gossip. Instead, my friends would tell me, "Every time we see you, your face gets cleaner and cleaner. " On this note, know who your friends are. Friends are encouraging and not derogatory. They lift you and should not put you down.

Even as a child, when I got quiet, my mom would think I was up to something. On the other hand, my daughter had a mature character for her age as a child, so it was customary not to worry about what she was doing when she was quiet. Amen. But unlike Jesus, as He grew up, His wisdom and stature increased, gaining the favor of God and man. But we all gain skeletons to hide in the closet as we grow up. As I am writing this, my daughter is working on her doctorate. I hope the best for her through her life experiences.

Jesus understood subjectivity, making it easier for Him to understand order; 1 Corinthians 14:40 (KJV) "Let all things be done decently and in order." Understanding that some applications are everlasting, the grounds for applying are different, called life understanding and life application.

When we see what we do is the Word of God, we call it spiritual application. You cannot run and have not learned how to walk. You cannot walk and do not know how to crawl, but there are exceptions to all rules. Enoch and Elisha went into heaven without seeing death; before Jesus Christ descended and ascended, their exception was what they already knew the way, who is Christ. However, their bodies had to transcend. Keep in mind that Jesus Christ was the first to descend and to ascend. When you know the things of God and have applied yourself, you will learn how to show yourself approved, even as Christ was approved.

All things born again in Christ are of God when appropriate in God. You need to not only allow the indwelling of the Holy Ghost, but your heart needs to submit to the Holy Ghost. In God, all things promised that are of God and by the Word of God are yours to claim.

Jesus had taken on our sins and had no sin. Jesus had shown himself worthy. I had to ask myself what it was that Jesus had allowed to shape and prune him, allowing his questions and answers to be so remarkable that these men called doctors in the temple were astonished, and not only them but all who heard him. Sometimes, close-minded people could get on your nerves and think they are correct. There are times when it has been a certain way for so long that people could be closed-minded and think they are right. Sometimes the old way of being right becomes obsolete, and the new correct way doesn't feel right. There are also times when change is difficult. Sometimes we conform to our way of doing things even when it's wrong after long periods. When new and correct ways become apparent, it could be a struggle. Sometimes, being wrong is not acknowledged until it is made known.

Jesus, at the age of twelve, had already learned to master conversation. He had already learned how to bring His vision across so that structure would not be an issue, that even the simple-minded would fully understand and not just the high-minded. Jesus deeply understood people at twelve and knew how not to get in His way. Jesus did not get this way without applied application. Please don't offer up only when it benefits you; as soon as you get struck down, you choose not to offer up anymore because you did not get your way. Also, you can't only show up because you have a vision and refuse to participate in approved works, especially due to anger. You must meet God where He is already working. How can you be dedicated to parenting your vision, saying God is, and not complying with God's Word? Jesus understood the scriptural application and knew where the Father needed Him.

Jesus was a parent of his calling and still understood the meaning of the covenant from childhood until adulthood. I have a ministry and am the parent of that ministry. But I still depend on my church home and its Pastor to be my covenant. We all need somebody to covenant with us. Being in Christ, we seek God's things; the best way to do this is to seek wisdom from God and spiritually mature Christians.

Rehoboam, the son of Salomon, we all know that Salomon was the wisest to have lived, yet his son chose to accept counseling from the inexperienced and not the experienced. Rehoboam did not seek after the covenant of God. God used Rehoboam as an instrument of destruction due to Salomon's disobedience with strange women to punish Israel by dividing the Israel nation into two kingdoms. **James** 4:10 (KJV) says, "Humble yourselves in the sight of the Lord, and he shall lift you up." When you line yourself up with the things of God, you are drawing nigh unto God. You will understand that humility is part of what God calls you to when you do this.

If anything is worth having, you will learn that it does not come easy. It would help if you processed learning. You may not be willing because the flesh is unwilling, but the spirit is. Understanding this is applying God's word to your life so that you might realize when to step back and ask God what the lesson is. Know that God is calling you to do something. Moses had stepped back and asked God, how can I lead your people when I am not eloquent? Moses had not realized that God had already trained him. Moses had to learn to endure to who he truly belonged to find his people. God knew Moses' name, and God is all-knowing, but for God to know you because you represent Him is a great pleasure.

Jesus, through all his opposition, had endured and did not waver. If you ask what Jesus would do, 1 Peter 5:9 (KJV)

[9.] "Whom resist stedfast in the faith, knowing that the same afflictions are accomplished in your brethren that are in the world.

"He resisted temptation and understood that no matter what, be about God's business. He kept the faith no matter what, and you should keep the faith.

If God is calling you and we all in Christ have a calling to the ministry of reconciliatio Whatever we are doing in Christ should be to God's glory. We don't shape our calling satisfy our friends. No, Jesus had many enemies, and He continues to be about God business. Jesus understood that those who chose to follow Him would have to endu persecution because He, the teacher, had to and that we all share in the suffering so that v may all rejoice together. Don't think that only you have a calling from the Lord, but we all d Don't think that what you have has never been done because then you are mistaken. Nothir is new under the sun and moon, and things happen redundantly per Ecclesiastes 1:9.

We want to see each other succeed in Christ, but some will fail because they are not obedie to God. There are those that the seeding of the Word has fallen on rocky ground. There a those whose seeding of the Word of God has fallen on shadow ground. There are tho whose seeding of the Word has felled on thrones. Then there are those that the seeding of th Word of God had fallen on good ground, as we are taught in the book of Mark and Matthe of the Bible. I ask the question of which of these you will reject and which of these you w receive. The choice is yours because God will have no man to perish, but man condem himself by their choices because of God's mercy and grace for our deliverance.

Mary and Joseph were worried sick when they could not find Jesus. God loves us like mother and a father. God doesn't want to see you going wrong. He wants you to understar that there is a way to all things. Sometimes you got to hold on and wait for that proper tim Our timing doesn't make it of God. I have had a vision since 1998. And over time, I began see how God works with my vision through God's provisioning. Some might say, well, tha you and not me, but I say what is of God shall come to pass. We must always look to whe God is working and wait on God. God knows and sees all, and He will provide for our need

1 Peter 5:6-8 (KJV)

6 Humble yourselves therefore under the mighty hand of God, that he may exalt you in d time:

7 Casting all your care upon him; for he careth for you.

Be sober, be vigilant; because your adversary the devil, as a roaring lion, walketh about, seeking whom he may devour:

I have learned what God has for me is for nobody but me. All I need to do is to allow God to prepare me through the process of ordaining me to what He calls me to. In other words, God said; first, I must take you through, then there is no other way to have greatness come out of it. I have learned that God knows God's business, and He could handle it better than I ever could or would. I had to learn that even in my humility, I must be sober and vigilant not to allow Satan to misdirect me, knowing that God will exalt me in the proper time, and all I need to do is wait and be willing. **1 Peter 5:10 (KJV)** "But the God of all grace, who hath called us unto his eternal glory by Christ Jesus, after that ye have suffered a while, make you perfect, establish, strengthen, settle *you*."

God invites us to help Him, and we must seek how. Nehemiah walked the broken wall before sharing his plan given to him by God's provisioning and then shared how and what is to be done. There are many body members, but only one body in Christ, and Christ is its' head. We are learning to work as one in Christ as one body. All ministries are profitable in the edification of the church.

Jesus did not say a word when He accepted His calling that He had on Him. He did not say a mumbling word. Now what we may be going through, imagine if He would have decided and said since I must suffer and then if it's my choice, I will not do it. Thank God for Jesus who had allowed himself to be humiliated, bruised, and beaten for our sake. He didn't have to do it. He could have said not me, but because He was about His father's business and not focus on any other matter that when taken on our sins and died, was buried, and rose again that His name was lifted above every name in heaven, on earth, and beneath the earth.

If you want what God calls you to, and have good fruit, let go and let God. Concern yourself with the things of God. Then give those matters to God because He gave them to you to steward over. Give them back to God for spiritual growth. When you tend to God's business He will take care of you. As David noted, I agree, pray, and wait on God. Jeremiah's 29th chapter teaches us that God's intentions for us are for good.

Caesar could not distract Jesus, the Pharisees and the Sadducees could not distract Jesus, Judas Iscariot could not distract Jesus, and yet Jesus did not turn His back on not one of them. God can take care of what He calls you to. We all must learn when, where, why, and how to get on board. Amen.

Mary knew how to hide the things that Jesus would say in her heart. We must allow the Holy Spirit, who not only dwells within us but also allows Him, to fill our spirits, both the young and the old.

CHAPTER THREE

The Way to Resurrection Through Christ (Spiritually and Physically)

Spiritual resurrection and a physical resurrection through Christ are possible. Here we are not talking about the 2nd Resurrection, who are the dead in Christ. We are talking about the saved in Christ and both their spiritual and physical resurrection, those who are made alive in Christ: quickened by the Holy Spirit being of the 1st Resurrection.

Spiritually Resurrected

If the Spirit of him that raised Jesus from the dead dwells in you, you are quickened in your spirit, being renewed of mind and heart. We are made new in Christ, now in a position to take on the things of God. The spiritual resurrection is to be empowered by the Holy Ghost of God to ward off what we were without God. We could not understand the things of God without the Holy Spirit working His ministry of sanctification in us. We learn who Jesus Christ is through the Holy Spirit. Jesus does not reveal to us who He is; Jesus we know through the third Godhead of the Trinity, God the Holy Spirit. 2 Corinthians 5:17-18 (KJV) "Therefore if any man be in Christ, he is a new creature: old things are passed away; behold, all things are become new. And all things are of God, who hath reconciled us to himself by Jesus Christ, and hath given to us the ministry of reconciliation."

Physically Resurrection

The Holy Spirit of God had raised the Son of God from the dead, shall also quicken our mortal bodies that dwelleth in us, Romans 8:11. The Holy Ghost that raised Jesus from the grave will physically raise the children of God from their grave. Our fate is part of our faith belief through obedience, and God's promise to us of eternal life. That is absolute salvation. Our fate depends on our confession of our believing faith that is absolute for salvation. Romans 10:9 (KJV) "That if thou shalt confess with thy mouth the Lord Jesus, and shalt believe in thine heart that God hath raised him from the dead, thou shalt be saved." For those in Christ, this takes place at the 1st Resurrection.

Labor of Deeds

When we labor for the Lord, we pray not to let our labor be in vain and to see the glory of the Lord with our own eyes. Jesus saw many the fruit of His seed when He rose on the third day from the grave. Jesus, in the flesh, was both man and God as the Son of man, the son of God has a divine spirit and a human nature, but we should remember that Jesus' human nature was whole being born of a virgin woman and not broken like we are as the fall of man by the act of Adam.

We will experience the same awakening from the grave when Jesus calls us to meet Him in the heavens.

Matthew 27:52-53 (KJV)

[52] And the graves were opened; and many bodies of the saints which slept arose,

[53] And came out of the graves after his Resurrection, and went into the holy city, and appeared unto many.

1 Corinthians 15:6-9 (KJV)

[6] After that, he was seen of above five hundred brethren at once; of whom the greater part remain unto this present, but some are fallen asleep.

[7] After that, he was seen of James; then of all the apostles.

[8] And last of all he was seen of me also, as of one born out of due time.

[9] For I am the least of the apostles, that am not meet to be called an apostle, because I persecuted the church of God.

Paul does not consider himself worthy of being an Apostle lightly but does not dismiss God's calling upon his life. Paul saw Jesus as did the Apostles. We should not so easily recognize being worthy or dismiss that God is Sovereign, doing as He pleases. All we are in God is credited to His mercy and grace.

Contemporary churches sometimes shape our minds to title ourselves by how we want to be characterized and dismiss God's focus. I have heard Christians say that they are under the Apostle so, and so. And to continue to say that they are the Apostle so and so followers. Christians are followers of Jesus Christ, our Lord, and Savior. We look to a spiritual head because it is God's order, but we are not followers of men. It's a big responsibility to be a spiritual leader. They should have a spirit of servitude and not a spirit of dictating and title importance. I say this not to discourage you but to enlighten you.

Christ In You

How is Jesus being God, able to die? Philippians 2:5-8 (KJV) "Let this mind be in you, which was also in Christ Jesus: Who, being in the form of God, thought it not robbery to be equal with God: But made himself of no reputation, and took upon him the form of a servant, and was made in the likeness of men: And being found in fashion as a man, he humbled himself, and became obedient unto death, even the death of the cross." Because He took on our sins and blotted out our sins, Jesus will not do this a second time. Death will not again touch the Lord. Understanding Jesus as God is the second Godhead of the Trinity; God the Son. Romans 6:9-10 (KJV)

[9] Knowing that Christ being raised from the dead dieth no more; death hath no more dominion over him.

[10] For in that he died, he died unto sin once: but in that he liveth, he liveth unto God.

We are not partially redeemed, but we are fully redeemed. (Noted: Jeremiah 31:33; Ezekiel 11:19,20; 36:26,27). It is because of the work of Christ on the Cross that we are made whole in God again. God gives us free will to choose to accept and follow Jesus Christ. Jesus took on the world's sins, and by acknowledging Jesus Christ and his blood that purchased the church of God, your sin is debtless. We become village people in Christ because of His blood. We become residents of the Kingdom of God.

But if we walk in the light, as he is in the light, we have fellowship one with another, and the blood of Jesus Christ his Son cleanseth us from all sin.

Hebrews 10:14-17 (KJV)

[14] For by one offering he hath perfected for ever them that are sanctified.

[15] *Whereof* the Holy Ghost also is a witness to us: for after that he had said before,

[16] This *is* the covenant that I will make with them after those days, saith the Lord, I will put my laws into their hearts, and in their minds will I write them;

[17] And their sins and iniquities will I remember no more.

Our spiritual Resurrection begins with Christ's physical death and His resurrection. Our spiritual learning starts with Christ's physical walk; we are followers of Christ: Christians are followers after Christ. I am talking about a spiritual rebirth because of Christ's sacrifice and bodily resurrection.

What is sin?

To disobey God and to walk contrary to God is a sin. God's love exceeds understanding. Knowing God's word teaches the things of God, and we learn to live His word through obedience. The only unforgivable sin is blasphemy against the Holy Spirit, which is a sin unto death. All sins are forgivable except for non-belief. So, to blasphemy, the Holy Spirit of God is to call God a liar since the Holy Spirit of God knows even the deepest thoughts of God. The Holy Spirit of God is the Spirit of Truth and knows the heart of God and men. Man's blasphemy of man is not an unforgivable sin. Jesus was a man born in the flesh by a virgin woman impregnated by the Holy Spirit. God is the other biological parent of Jesus. God the Father is the first person of the Godhead. Matthew 12:31-32 (KJV)"Wherefore I say unto you, All manner of sin and blasphemy shall be forgiven unto men: but the blasphemy against the

Holy Ghost shall not be forgiven unto men. And whosoever speaketh a word against the Son of man, it shall be forgiven him: but whosoever speaketh against the Holy Ghost, it shall not be forgiven him, neither in this world, neither in the world to come."

Joshua dedicates a lifestyle to work out, study, do, walk, practice, love, exalt, witness, testify, teach, (as for my house (Joshua 24:15). Your lifestyle is shaped by how you yield to the Holy Spirit. How you study, what you study, how you meditate, and how you pray. Hebrews 4:11 (KJV) "Let us labour therefore to enter into that rest, lest any man fall after the same example of unbelief" and James 2:17 (KJV) "Even so faith, if it hath not works, is dead, being alone."

Psalm 27:14 (KJV)

Jesus showed us, when walking with the 12 Apostles and Paul, the last Apostle of God, the love of God. Jesus' faithfulness and loving-kindness through his death, burial, and resurrection did send back the one baptizing with fire. He is the comforter, the third Godhead: God the Holy Spirit, who teaches and empowers us of the things of God. His ministry is the ministry of sanctification.

Holy Ghost Empowerment

We recognize the Trinity as the Triune God: Being three in ONE:

God the Father, God the Son, and God the Holy Ghost. Three persons in one Being. The Godhead. By the Holy Spirit, we are given an understanding of this knowledge. We learn to love God as clay, with God being the Potter as the Father. We know that God blessed us with the Promised Seed, our Savior. We also understand God as Creator.

Put into proper perspective with proper proportion: God the Creator could do and be whatever He chose. Here is a teaching that might at first sound contrary to what we thought we already knew. Without God, there would be no Jesus, the Son of Man, the Son of God. "In the beginning was the Word, and the Word was with God, and the Word was God" (John 1:1). But some say there is no God without Jesus because they are the same. To believe that is to misbelieve in the order of God. The correct order is to think that there is no Jesus without God. Our predestination back to God begins with God the Creator. Yet, the Word and the Spirit of God are God.

Jesus coming in the flesh is after the fact that God had chosen to predestine us back to Himself. God made His Word to be Jesus, thus making Him in the flesh and the Second Person of the Godhead manifested itself. God put into force the New Testament as the third covenant when He did this. The first covenant is the Rainbow symbol to remember not to destroy the world with water again. The second covenant was with Abraham by circumcision in the Old Testament for the Jew culture. The Ten Commandments is not a covenant but allowed man to see that he was in sin and needed a Savior, which brings us to the third covenant. Jesus says this is my body and my blood of the New Testament.

Jesus being God purchased the church with His blood (Acts 20:28). God continues to build the church, even today (Mathew 16:18), Chief Shepard (1Peter 5:4), and the Good Shepard (John 10: 11,14). God never leaves His throne, and with God, nothing is impossible for Him.

Yes, because of this, Jesus is also God, but in proper perspective, God the Creator was before He made His Word, who was God and was with God to be Jesus in the flesh. God could have chosen not to have emptied Himself into the flesh, whom we know as Jesus Christ, our Lord, and Savior. Thank God for being so humbled that we know Him today as God the Father, Son, and Holy Ghost (Philippians 2:7), but we must not forget God the Creator. God's choice "and the Word was made flesh, and dwelt among us, (and we beheld his glory, the glory as of the only begotten of the Father,) full of grace and truth" John 1:14 (KJV).

God the Creator saw the fruit of His seed before the foundation of the world was created. God is omniscient, omnipresent, and omnipotent.

Romans 8:29 (KJV)

[29] For whom he did foreknow, he also did predestinate *to be* conformed to the image of his Son, qa2that he might be the firstborn among many brethren.

Ephesians 1:4-14 (KJV)

[4] According as he hath chosen us in him before the foundation of the world, that we should be holy and without blame before him in love:

[5] Having predestinated us unto the adoption of children by Jesus Christ to himself, according to the good pleasure of his will,

[6] To the praise of the glory of his grace, wherein he hath made us accepted in the beloved.

[7] In whom we have redemption through his blood, the forgiveness of sins, according to the riches of his grace;

[8] Wherein he hath abounded toward us in all wisdom and prudence;

[9] Having made known unto us the mystery of his will, according to his good pleasure which he hath purposed in himself:

[10] That in the dispensation of the fulness of times he might gather together in one all things in Christ, both which are in heaven, and which are on earth; *even* in him:

[11] In whom also we have obtained an inheritance, being predestinated according to the purpose of him who worketh all things after the counsel of his own will:

[12] That we should be to the praise of his glory, who first trusted in Christ.

[13] In whom ye also *trusted*, after that ye heard the word of truth, the gospel of your salvation: in whom also after that ye believed, ye were sealed with that holy Spirit of promise,

[14] Which is the earnest of our inheritance until the redemption of the purchased possession, unto the praise of his glory.

As a disciple of the Lord. Who you are is reflected by how you study, pray, and meditate. Your memories make you who you are, and your mind will take you to where your heart is.

Matthew 6:21 (HCSB) "For where your treasure is, there your heart will be also." You must learn to keep your mind on God's things daily, always creating memories and life experiences to connect with God.

The Holy Spirit quickens spiritually and physically, being made alive in the flesh as a newborn creature because we have accepted Jesus Christ as our Lord and Savior. As the Holy Spirit raised Jesus from the grave because of His blood, we are made new being resurrected in Christ (2 Corinthians 5:17-21) and are sealed by the Holy Spirit as children of God. In Christ, being raised from the grave, God gives us a new body (2Corinthians 5:1), "We know that if the earthly tent we live in is torn down, we have a building in heaven that comes from God, an eternal house not built by human hands" (ISV).

CHAPTER FOUR

Attitude In Christ

Depending on your attitude, you succeed at different levels of whom you are serving. Two ways things enter the body. The first is by substance: food, liquid, injection, or air, and the second is knowledge: understanding, experiences, and wisdom. Anything that digests cannot defile the body. Knowledge can spoil you, but it depends on your attitude toward Christ. Your heart is the filter of what you put out. It reveals you. In general, how you study becomes who you are and who you are, becomes a lifestyle.

Mark 7:20-23 (KJV)

[20] And he said, That which cometh out of the man, that defileth the man.

[21] For from within, out of the heart of men, proceed evil thoughts, adulteries, fornications, murders,

[22] Thefts, covetousness, wickedness, deceit, lasciviousness, an evil eye, blasphemy, pride, foolishness:

[23] All these evil things come from within, and defile the man.

Matthew 6:21-23 (KJV)

21 For where your treasure is, there will your heart be also.

22 The light of the body is the eye: if therefore thine eye be single, thy whole body shall be full of light.

23 But if thine eye be evil, thy whole body shall be full of darkness. If therefore the light that is in thee be darkness, how great is that darkness!

Stubbornness Vs. Immaturity

A stubborn man comes as being all-knowing and not as a child. He is rigid in his ways, and his faith he has none but proceeds with his wit. Christians should come to understand the things of God, and this is too hard for the unjust to distinguish between error and truth. Stubbornness is witchcraft and accompanies the pride of life, which does not come from God. Luke 18:17 (KJV) "Verily I say unto you, Whosoever shall not receive the kingdom of God as a little child shall in no wise enter therein." We must come willing to learn of God as little children. Wisdom starts with knowing God. In Christ we are reborn, and all babies must be taught as they grow. We must learn the things that are of God. All these things to us are new.

Stubbornness is intentional. Immaturity is unintentional. However, you can accompany stubbornness with immaturity, and submission leads to maturity by choice. Choosing what you submit to give in to is your choice. To paint a clear picture is to say it becomes who you are. Stubbornness is hearing God's Word but not feeling its power due to the lack of submission to the Holy Ghost of God. The Holy Ghost gives us the ability to experience God. This is called experiencing God. This cannot happen without the Holy Ghost. The ministry of the Holy Ghost is to sanctify us, teaching us the things of God. Being under the blood of Jesus Christ we are consecrated for the workings of God. The closer you draw to God, the deeper your love grows in Him. He blesses the righteous, and the unrighteous will be judged.

Exodus 32:9-10 (KJV)

"And the LORD said unto Moses, I have seen this people, and, behold, it *is* a stiffnecked people:⁰ Now therefore let me alone, that my wrath may wax hot against them, and that I may consume them: and I will make of thee a great nation" (Jews and Gentiles are both included in this promise renewed with Moses, God made to Abraham.)

Romans 1:16 (KJV) "For I am not ashamed of the gospel of Christ: for it is the power of God unto salvation to every one that believeth; to the Jew first, and also to the Greek."

Stubborn attributes and pride are turning up your nose, hard-headedness, intentionally selective hearing, and rolling your eyes at the truth as a child who rebels against teachers and parents. Stubbornness is making incidents of others as if they are the problem while failing to see themselves as thick-headedness. Jeremiah 5:21 (KJV) "Hear now this, O foolish people, and without understanding; which have eyes, and see not; which have ears, and hear not:" Lost in your own causes, hindering of your own growth, hampered, or impeded by your own ways and thoughts. 2 Corinthians 6:12 (KJV) "Ye are not straitened in us, but ye are straitened in your own bowels." Walking by their own knowledge and disregarding what is of God. Disregarding the truth and not being able to comprehend it. Jealous of those who walk in deep wisdom given by God. These are all forms of big-headedness and pride.

Looking at stubbornness universally, Israel wanted to do things while being in the desert by their timing and not God's way. They refuse to trust in God even after having to experience God's power as a people. They could not enter the Promise Land because of their way, except for Joshua, the younger generation, and Caleb. Everybody in Christ came or is coming with a mind for learning, as a child would. Matthew 18:3 (KJV) "And said, Verily I say unto you, Except ye be converted, and become as little children, ye shall not enter into the kingdom of heaven."

Submission: 1 Thessalonians 4:11; 2 Corinthians 12:5; Proverbs 3:5

Submission comes with obedience, and obedience comes with instructions. 1 Thessalonians 4:11 (KJV) "And that ye study to be quiet, and to do your own business, and to work with your own hands, as we commanded you;"

Paul knew how to mind his own. Now listen to what the Bible says. Everybody in the Bible that wanted to be equal to God got into soul-seeking trouble—naming a few: Satan (Isaiah 14:12-14), Adam, Pharaohs (kings of Egypt), Kings (such as Nebuchadnezzar), the beast (political systems), man (like a man of power), The Anti-Christ (the imitator of Christ), and anybody else that want to be equal to God. We must strive to be more like God, but we do this through being who we are in Christ.

[2] Genesis 3:4-7 (KJV)

And the serpent said unto the woman, Ye shall not surely die:

For God doth know that in the day ye eat thereof, then your eyes shall be opened, and ye shall be as gods, knowing good and evil.

[6] And when the woman saw that the tree *was* good for food, and that it *was* pleasant to the eyes, and a tree to be desired to make *one* wise, she took of the fruit thereof, and did eat, and gave also unto her husband with her; and he did eat.

[7] And the eyes of them both were opened, and they knew that they *were* naked; and they sewed fig leaves together, and made themselves aprons.

Daniel 4:30-31 (KJV)

[30] The king spake, and said, Is not this great Babylon, that I have built for the house of the kingdom by the might of my power, and for the honour of my majesty?

[31] While the word *was* in the king's mouth, there fell a voice from heaven, *saying*, O king Nebuchadnezzar, to thee it is spoken; The kingdom is departed from thee.

Like Paul, I do not want to be equal to God. I can't be God if I wanted to, and God couldn't be me if He wanted to because He cannot sin; I can. I can't be Christ even if I wanted to because Christ is sinless, and I'm not. I desire to be transformed, renewed, and forgiven. I want to be with God. I want to be in Christ. Because I wanted to be above my sinful nature, I chose to follow Christ. I want to be Christ-like, but I don't want to be anybody but who I am. You cannot be any of those things in Christ, wanting to be like man, which is to idolize. Christ was a man also, and there is a difference between being like Christ and Christ-like. Christ-like means having something in common with God's righteousness. And to have the likeness of character, you need to put on the things of God while being yourself.

2 Corinthians 12:5 (KJV)

[5] "Of such an one will I glory: yet of myself I will not glory, but in mine infirmities."

Work to make your life in Christ known to others but be humble and always give God the glory. In other words, if you live a saved life, then it will be noticeable. Like what the song says, "Have You Been Tried by The Fire."

"If you really been converted,

You don't mind letting the whole world know,

But you really don't have to tell it,

If you live it, the world will know."

Proverbs 3:5 (KJV)

[5] "Trust in the LORD with all thine heart; and lean not unto thine own understanding."

Immaturity

Depending on your attitude, your heart shows who you are. Matthew 6:21 (KJV) "For where your treasure is, there will your heart be also.

"There is a lady that takes her anger out by raging at others. Her heart is driven by hurt and causes others to share her pain.

Sin works through spiritual forces that invade our nature to its core. It operates through spiritual oppression and spiritual possession.

Spiritual Oppression: prolonged cruel or unjust treatment or control that must be submitted to. Spiritual possession: an unusual or altered state of consciousness and associated behaviors purportedly caused by taking authority of a human body by spirits.

1 Corinthians 13:11 (KJV)

[11] "When I was a child, I spake as a child, I understood as a child, I thought as a child: but when I became a man, I put away childish things.

"The immature blames others and refuses to take responsibility for their actions and reactions. We see a great example of spiritual immaturity in Genesis 3:11-13 (HCSB)

[11] Then He asked, "Who told you that you were naked? Did you eat from the tree that I commanded you not to eat from?"

[12] Then the man replied, "The woman You gave to be with me—she gave me [some fruit] from the tree, and I ate."

[13] So the LORD God asked the woman, "What is this you have done?" And the woman said, "It was the serpent. He deceived me, and I ate."

The closer you are to God, the more spiritually mature you are. Those who are under the blood of Jesus cannot be spiritually possessed. However, they could be spiritually oppressed. Spiritual oppression could only come by your submission to take control over you. In Christ, oppression is by submitting, be careful what you are feeding spiritually on. But the children of God are protected because of the blood of Jesus from demons. The closer you are to God, the stronger your faith and practicing faith. What you choose to practice becomes your input to who you are and to what you are submitting unto.

Those not of God cannot wade off spiritual oppression or spiritual possession. Those who are not in Christ can be possessed involuntarily. And some devote themselves by submission to the evil spirit. They are Satan's disciples.

Aam and Eve were not disciples of Satan, but they submitted to Satan's directions over God's directions and because of that we too are born under the order of sin. Satan infiltrated human nature when Adam touched and ate the fruit from the Tree of Knowledge of good and evil. Adam had no idea what evil was prior to his choice. He did not fully realize the evil of Satan, but he just knew Satan because Satan would be in the Garden of Eden. Sometimes you need to remove yourself from certain environments or from certain associations to make better choices. You even may need to leave your residence or general locality, neighborhood, or community to live a better life, "and be not conformed to this world: but be ye transformed by the renewing of your mind, that you may prove what is that good and acceptable and perfect will of God" (Romans 12:2 KJV). 2 Corinthians 6:17 (KJV) says, "Wherefore come out from among them, and be ye separate, saith the Lord, and touch not the unclean thing; and I will receive you." Your habitat is your personal Garden of Eden.

God left Adam with a right of choice to choose to obey Him. God told Adam what not to do and what to do and did not slander even Satan. Yet Satan had slandered God. You should be careful with whom you build relationships. If they are talking with you about somebody, then be fully aware of them being themselves.

Titus 3:2 (KJV)

[2] "To speak evil of no man, to be no brawlers, *but* gentle, shewing all meekness unto all men." God is all-knowing and cannot sin, so Scripture does not contradict itself. Satan had set up Adam as a breach to enter into the nature of all men, the seed of Adam. Adam was the gatekeeper of his sperm. Satan became a part of Adam's nature when Satan oppressed Adam. Adam allowed this to happen.

It was Adam's seed that Satan was after. For instance, if Adam had children with concubines, they too would be the seed of Adam. All men are born in sin by nature because of Adam's choice. Adam was the first man, and no other man was the first. Adam's name is "Son of the red earth," the first human. Adam knew evil now by Satan being a part of his nature through oppression. Adam was too close to God for Satan to control him by possession, but his seed could be possessed and oppressed. Satan was making human nature broken and divided between good and evil. When Adam gave in to Satan, he allowed Satan's division and disobedience to work sin in us. Sin is a spiritual work in our nature. Satan found a way to marry into humankind to possess God's creation. Today men teach through socialism and the system the means to be oppressed. Today mankind, his human nature is involuntarily possessed and choosing to be voluntarily oppressed.

Ephesians 6:12 (KJV)

[12] "For we wrestle not against flesh and blood, but against principalities, against powers, against the rulers of the darkness of this world, against spiritual wickedness in high *places*."

2 Corinthians 4:3-4 (KJV) "But if our gospel be hid, it is hid to them that are lost:

[4] In whom the god of this world hath blinded the minds of them which believe not, lest the light of the glorious gospel of Christ, who is the image of God, should shine unto them."

We must be born again to divorce Satan and let a divorce be a divorce. We must be enlightened with a new nature, not married to the devil and his will. We must now put on the Armor of God and discern the things of God.

John 3:5-7 (KJV)

[5] Jesus answered, Verily, verily, I say unto thee, Except a man be born of water and *of* the Spirit, he cannot enter into the kingdom of God.

[6] That which is born of the flesh is flesh; and that which is born of the Spirit is spirit.

[7] Marvel not that I said unto thee, Ye must be born again.

We must not go back to the ways of the old, which is to be bonded again to sin when we are freed. God gave us the way.

Luke 9:62 (KJV)

[62] "And Jesus said unto him, No man, having put his hand to the plough, and looking back, is fit for the kingdom of God." We must move on with our new life in Christ. We are with a new nature being of God once we are freed from the bondage of sin.

Romans 12:2 (BBE)

[2] "And let not your behaviour be like that of this world, but be changed and made new in mind, so that by experience you may have knowledge of the good and pleasing and complete purpose of God.

2 Corinthians 6:14 (BBE)

[14] "Do not keep company with those who have not faith: for what is there in common between righteousness and evil, or between light and dark?"

The closer you are to God, the more spiritually mature you are to become.

A child is without sound reasoning. A child does not know enough to have a good understanding. A child throws tantrums and outbursts with the first thing that comes to mind. A child does not think through their hurt. A child does not know how to handle feelings. They are not in control of their intentions, and how could they be? The immature become angry when they do not have their way and when you tell them what they need to hear, they think you should agree in their favor.

Immaturity is Unintentional in the Ways of Being Childish

Hebrews 5:13 (KJV)

[13] "For every one that useth milk *is* unskilful in the word of righteousness: for he is a babe." Listen, feelings are secondary to spiritual knowledge – meaning to study, have devotion, and apply the Word of God and not be led by your emotions, or logic, or science. You should put all things into perspective by seeking first the Kingdom of God, and then those other things may follow if appropriate. Your feelings can be misleading, but to seek God is not misleading.

Unskillful in the word of righteousness is to know just enough to be dangerous, as well as not knowing the enemy at all. The difference is that being in Christ you are protected as you learn the things that are of God. The unskilled have not learned how to interpret with understanding—how to apply what is being read or heard—how to practice application study—knowing Scripture but having no wisdom or revelation—not being able to establish a foundation—not able to focus and being given too many directions. Being confused and puzzled about who your friends are or not, and unable to stand on God's word alone and to understand inner battles (spiritual things).

Being a babe in Christ gives their immaturity an advantage over ignorance as they grow in Christ. The positive about being immature while being a babe in Christ is to come as a child, ready to learn. They are being active in God's word. Being a babe in Christ is one of the key preparations to enter into the Kingdom of God.

Stubbornness Accompany by Immaturity

Stubbornness by choice invites immaturity as the alternative to what you are practicing. Jeremiah 5:21-22 (KJV) [1] "Hear now this, O foolish people, and without understanding; which have eyes, and see not; which have ears, and hear not: Fear ye not me? saith the LORD: will ye not tremble at my presence, which have placed the sand *for* the bound of the sea by a perpetual decree, that it cannot pass it: and though the waves thereof toss themselves, yet can they not prevail; though they roar, yet can they not pass over it?"

The choice to be stubborn will prevent you from spiritual growth. When you choose stubbornness, you place yourself in a position to impede maturity. Refusing to listen does not mean you do not hear. It comes in one ear and goes out the other when this happens, so you are hearing, but nothing settles in you to make a great foundation. It would be best if you learned to listen to what you hear and seek understanding.

God is talking to his creation, and it is not hearing Him. How long has God been talking to you, and you keep not hearing Him? No matter if He is speaking to you through circumstances, prayer, somebody, or your experiences are you listening and seeking understanding?

Seeing without seeing is refusing to learn by the examples you are experiencing. You keep going back to the same drawing board, so your results always end up indifferent to what you seek. You find yourself making the same mistakes over and over. Also, you find yourself making the mistakes of others. You do not accomplish better means because you refuse to process or consider your life experiences for the better. So, you accompany stubbornness with immaturity in your endings and your beginnings. Intentional foolishness becomes the pattern of who you are. Your outputs are the result of your inputs. Many factors go within, and only one person becomes of it and then another. Again, your outputs are the result of your information and then there are two and three. Man teaches man the means to being oppressed and to enjoy it. This is deceitfulness. The devil is a liar, and the truth is not in him.

John 8:43-44 (KJV)

[43] Why do ye not understand my speech? *even* because ye cannot hear my word.

[44] Ye are of *your* father the devil, and the lusts of your father ye will do. He was a murderer from the beginning, and abode not in the truth, because there is no truth in him. When he speaketh a lie, he speaketh of his own: for he is a liar, and the father of it.

Maturity

Hebrews 5:14 (KJV)

[14] "But strong meat belongeth to them that are of full age, *even* those who by reason of use have their senses exercised to discern both good and evil." God's word must come first, and if it leads to being accompanied by your feelings, logic, and science, then okay and not the other way around.

I remember when being in the military, we had a live-fire exercise. I was the point man. We were entering the tree line within the forest, and cross-firing started about 30 yards in front of us. We watched tracers and listened to bullets smacking the trees. Just three seconds before the firing, I stopped. Something told me to stop. The squad would not move without my lead. The squad leader demanded that I go forward doing those 3 seconds before the firing started but ceased ordering until after the shooting. We went forward. When it was time to go back out, the men consulted with me should they go back out. Depending on what I said, even if they were court-martial, they would do as I suggested. I thought to myself, I can't let that happen. I said yes, go, and they went. As for me, I noticed that there was something about me, but only for a moment. I had other experiences when I saw that I had more authority than those that outranked me in certain instances. I never use it for my selfishness but always for the better benefit of others. So, in our shared experiences, we see them and me being mature and, secondly, the men putting their logic second to what was a spiritual incident, including myself. Putting your feelings, reasoning, or science first is not spiritual maturity and could be misleading.

Matthew 6:22 (KJV)

22 The light of the body is the eye: if therefore thine eye be single, thy whole body shall be full of light.

Matthew 6:33 (KJV)

33 But seek ye first the kingdom of God, and his righteousness; and all these things shall be added unto you.

Proverbs 3:5-6 (KJV)

5 Trust in the LORD with all thine heart; and lean not unto thine own understanding.

6 In all thy ways acknowledge him, and he shall direct thy paths.

Remember, there are two ways for spiritual warfare to enter the body: physically and mentally. Remember, anything that is digested does not defile the body but can make you sick. The combination of your body, heart, and mind is the filter to what you feed on, physically or mentally. What goes in must come out. Spirits can enter physically or mentally. Because you are in Christ and protected by a spiritual seal, you have the power of God to resist oppression when you submit to God. However, if you are not careful to submit to God, you could permit yourself to be oppressed by evil spirits. On the other hand, possession is without permission to control you when you are not under the blood. You are powerless to resist Satan without Christ. Your heart is the filter of what you are feeding on. It reveals you.

CHAPTER FIVE

The Account

Romans 14:12 (KJV)

[12] "So then every one of us shall give account of himself to God."

Every single soul must give an account of every act, word, and thought that is done in life, in the body.

Are we in control of our thoughts, and if not, why is it required to give an account when we are not in control of all our thoughts, which is a pervasive question we may ask? Principalities, powers, evil rulers, and spiritual wickedness generate images, ideas, and matters of your mind. We can't control what enters our minds, or what we may see or hear in life, but sometimes we can. Yet, you oversee what you do with all your thoughts, even the thoughts you didn't put there, yes. Reading James 4:7 (KJV), "Submit yourselves therefore to God. Resist the devil, and he will flee from you", we see that we are empowered to submit unto or to resist temptation. Empowerment comes by studying to know your relationship with God through the Word and your experiences with God. Your relationship with God is guided by the Holy Ghost who resides within you. The Holy Ghost gives you all of Him, but how much of you are you giving to the Holy Ghost?

The Three Points

Let's summarize the three points in James 4:7: submit, resist, and deliverance.

These are weapons from God to godly man because only the righteous of God is equipped to evoke God's will into their life. It is the precious Spirit of God that enables us to remember the things of God. In our life experiences, we are fortunate to know God. Our decisions on matters should be by having our minds on God. The flesh is unwilling to satisfy God, but our spirit does please God. The faithful men of God confirm the struggle of life temptations as we read through the bible; even Jesus expressed this between His prayers (Matthew 26:41) in the Garden of Gethsemane.

We must learn to submit and resist for deliverance. We do this by being led in Christ by the empowering Spirit of God, which we know as the Holy Spirit. We usually learn through prayer, meditation, devotion, studying, and application. The children of God could gain these through personal or impersonal experiences. The book of 2 Corinthians 5: 2-5 and Romans 12:2 speaks about transforming your deeds to be of God so that life may be your reward in the presence of God.

Two Foundations: (no in-between, no gray areas, no straddling the fence)

The Foundation of the Believer (Righteous)

The foundation of the believer we know as God the Son, which is the second Godhead of the Triune God. The first is God the Father, and the third is God the Holy Spirit. The believer's foundation is having faith in God's plan through the Son of God. The Son of God is the actual son of our Heavenly Father. His name is Jesus Christ, Emanuel. He is also the son of man, born of flesh but by a virgin woman impregnated by the Holy Spirit. His mother's name was Mary, and his stepfather was Joseph. Joseph had not yet known his wife, Mary. The child came to be the atonement of men's sins. He was persecuted by men and died on the cross. His death on the cross lifted the cross from the lowest form of persecution to the highest. While on the cross, he was pierced with a spear. Water and blood had poured out of Him. He was without sin, yet He took on the world's sin. A sufficient sacrifice for God to forgive men. Jesus was buried in a borrowed grave. He rose from that grave on the third day and is now with the Heavenly Father. We learn of this in the readings of the four Gospels: Matthew, Mark, Luke, and John. To believe and accept Jesus as Lord and Savior is the believer's foundation. The sin that leads not unto death is a sinner that chooses to believe.

Being a believer exempts you from sin wages. You are no longer a sinner because your mind and your heart now desire the things that are of God. You are still subjected to sin because of the flesh. You are always forgiven because of the blood of Jesus. Paul explains that the sins that we do are not our sins to claim. The desire is putting God first, loving God, and desiring God. We are new creatures in Christ, not bound by the flesh or our old nature. 1 John 3:9 (BBE) "Anyone who is a child of God does no sin, because he still has God's seed in him; he is not able to be a sinner, because God is his Father." If the King says you are pardoned, then so be it. God, the King is a just and righteous Father who will not be deceived. Do not become the sin that you are capable of being caught up in. There is a difference between being caught up in sin and becoming that sin you are caught up in. God knows the heart of all men. Pray that your heart is of God. (STOP AND PRAY).

But we do get caught up in ungodliness from time to time. Jesus also came to understand how our flesh could be affected by our sinful nature, yet Jesus had a different nature. Before Adam had descended humankind into sin, Adam's nature was of a divine status as is Jesus. Thank God that Jesus succeeded in the flesh where Adam failed. This is why we call Jesus, the second Adam. We were all born sinners by nature, so we are born in sin. Jesus is the propitiation for our sins, and the penalty for sin is paid in full for those who follow Jesus Christ. 1 Corinthians 15:45 (KJV) "And so it is written, The first man Adam was made a living soul; the last Adam *was made* a quickening spirit."

The Foundation of the non-believer (Unrighteous)

Those who walk not according to God are to understand its reason. It is not something that we can choose to do on our own. Romans 8:7-8 (BBE)

"Because the mind of the flesh is opposite to God; it is not under the law of God, and is not able to be: So that those who are in the flesh are not able to give pleasure to God." There is an inner strength that only God can provide for us to take on the character of God, and without the Holy Spirit, there is no understanding of God. The ministry of the Holy Spirit to sanctify the children of God. God and Jesus are revealed to us through the Ministry of Sanctification, which is the ministry of the Holy Spirit. This is begun in the sinner as a sinner being guided or prep for their conversion.

There is a basic understanding of the foundation of the non-believer: the sin that leads to death and not life. 1 John 5:17 (KJV) "All unrighteousness is sin: and there is a sin not unto death." The sin that leads to death is blasphemy, which is unbelief. They do not believe in the Son of God to be who He says He is and that He is the world's savior because they reject the Holy Spirit, who testifies 0f Him, or those who continually put off what they do know to be true. What is "sin unto death": (disbelief and unjustified by the blood of Jesus) To die during a sinful life.

Matthew 12:30-32 (KJV)

30 He that is not with me is against me; and he that gathereth not with me scattereth abroad.

31 Wherefore I say unto you, All manner of sin and blasphemy shall be forgiven unto men: but the blasphemy against the Holy Ghost shall not be forgiven unto men.

32 And whosoever speaketh a word against the Son of man, it shall be forgiven him: but whosoever speaketh against the Holy Ghost, it shall not be forgiven him, neither in this world, neither in the world to come.

We should not pray for forgiveness or mercy for those who are in the state of sin, choosing to practice sin or to remain in sin. We should pray that they are delivered from their state of sin. Then when they are delivered, they are no longer intentional in their state.

1 John 5:5-6 (KJV)

5 Who is he that overcometh the world, but he that believeth that Jesus is the Son of God?

6 This is he that came by water and blood, even Jesus Christ; not by water only, but by water and blood. And it is the Spirit that beareth witness, because the Spirit is truth.

Two Categories of Deeds: Godly and Ungodly

Godly Deeds

God will reward godly deeds which go beyond the Gift of God, which is life. The Law kills when it is lonely, and Faith is empty when it is lonely. When living by the Law, even if you are successful with 9 out of 10, it is because of the lack of one that you are guilty of them all. When claiming faith is void of works, you are guilty of faithlessness. The Law must have faith as a company, as well as faith must have the Law to accompany it (James 2:14-26).

Both mercy and grace produce faith in your life. God is the initiator of all things and merciful to whom He chooses. Faith before works because it is faith that credit works and then works that credits faith. Your actions prove faith. Hebrews 11:1 (KJV) "Now faith is the substance of things hoped for, the evidence of things not seen." Faith alone is not credited with believing when there is no obedience to God. There are many working things coming together when understanding to obey God. 1 John 5:18 (KJV) "We know that whosoever is born of God sinneth not; but he that is begotten of God keepeth himself, and that wicked one toucheth him not." Those who are of God will desire the things of God. God's children receive the ministry of the Holy Spirit working within. The Ministry of the Holy Spirit is sanctification. He works in our hearts the law of God, and those that love God will keep his law. Children of God grow spiritually mature as they walk with God like a newborn with their parents.

Ungodly Deeds

Anybody that does good deeds when coming from the heart, that deed is classified as being godly, but only being under the blood will guarantee that you are not punished for your sins. But you know the tree by the fruit it bears. All men should give an account for both good and bad works: Romans 14:12 (KJV) "So then every one of us shall give account of himself to God."

Matthew 7:17-19 (KJV)

17 Even so every good tree bringeth forth good fruit; but a corrupt tree bringeth forth evil fruit.

18 A good tree cannot bring forth evil fruit, neither can a corrupt tree bring forth good fruit.

19 Every tree that bringeth not forth good fruit is hewn down, and cast into the fire.

Some may appeal to have good intentions, but their motive is evil. Ultimately, the punishment for sin is death and not life, so the difference between the two is those who are saved from sins will be forgiven. Still, we all shall be judged for our deeds, rather good or evil. The ultimate and general reward for all of God's children is life eternal. No matter their deeds, the unforgiven shall suffer loss in the Lake of Fire and Brimstone.

They are not subjected to God's things (Romans 8:7).

Walking In Judgment

We are walking in judgment, proving the things of God (Romans 12:2), meaning that we are being chastised, established, and settled so that we can have a good report and be rewarded for our deeds at the judgment seat of Jesus Christ. God's children are the world's light (Matthew 5:14-16). God told Moses to stand next to Him on a rock, and He will put him in a clef to hide Moses from seeing His face but not His back to know His glory (Exodus 33:19-22). Jesus came as the rock of salvation and showed us His face so that we may know the Father. We become followers of Christ, our Lord, and Savoir, and the world through us might know Jesus. We have a merciful and graceful God to thank for this opportunity.

Those who can please God are of God. They are washed and made white as snow because of the Son of God. Children of God will lose branches but shall stand as a tree with its roots in Him. The child of God shall be saved. The things in us that are not of the Father shall be removed from us. Again, this is the ministry of the Holy Spirit of God working within us. Our branches bear good fruit because of the indwelling of the Comforter that teaches and reminds us of the things of God. How we submit to the Holy Spirit, set our spiritual growth speed.

John 15:1-7 (KJV)

1 I am the true vine, and my Father is the husbandman.

2 Every branch in me that beareth not fruit he taketh away: and every branch that beareth fruit, he purgeth it, that it may bring forth more fruit.

3 Now ye are clean through the word which I have spoken unto you.

4 Abide in me, and I in you. As the branch cannot bear fruit of itself, except it abide in the vine; no more can ye, except ye abide in me.

5 I am the vine, ye are the branches: He that abideth in me, and I in him, the same bringeth forth much fruit: for without me ye can do nothing.

6 If a man abide not in me, he is cast forth as a branch, and is withered; and men gather them, and cast them into the fire, and they are burned.

7 If ye abide in me, and my words abide in you, ye shall ask what ye will, and it shall be done unto you.

Abiding In Truth: Confidence

Christ is the Word. Christ is the Gospel. Christ is the Way. Christ is the Light. Christ is the Living Waters. Christ is the Truth. Sanctification is by the Spirit of the Holy Ghost, who reveals to us Christ and then works within us God's sanctifying grace through His son, by the revealing of His Spirit, who teaches us all things in decency and orderly. God gives us one chance after another chance to please Him through holiness. 1 Peter 1:16 "Because it is written, Be ye holy; for I am holy."

God gives us confidence in Salvation while running this race.

Hebrews 10:10-17 (KJV)

10 By the which will we are sanctified through the offering of the body of Jesus Christ once for all.

11 And every priest standeth daily ministering and offering oftentimes the same sacrifices, which can never take away sins:

12 But this man, after he had offered one sacrifice for sins for ever, sat down on the right hand of God;

13 From henceforth expecting till his enemies be made his footstool.

14 For by one offering he hath perfected for ever them that are sanctified.

15 Whereof the Holy Ghost also is a witness to us: for after that he had said before,

16 This is the covenant that I will make with them after those days, saith the Lord, I will put my laws into their hearts, and in their minds will I write them;

17 And their sins and iniquities will I remember no more.

Abiding in the Word and the Word abiding in you gives you the ability to ride God's wave link of grace (John 15:7). Those who are not abiding in the Word of God are being overtaken by the matters of the world (John 15:6). God will judge you in the truth of what you deserve. God will judge you by your overall character: mind, heart, and acts as a whole.

The carnal-minded in Christ are not choosing to become skilled in the things that are of God to do. They have the power to make godly decisions, but they refuse to be spiritually minded enough to become spiritually mature. You remain as babes in Christ, having only a heart of ready flesh because you want to do good but refuse to put yourself in the garden. In Christ, God takes away our hearts of stone, gives us a heart of flesh (Jeremiah 30:31), and puts His commandments on it.

God allows us to thirst after His will by giving us a new spirit of our hearts. Our minds and our hearts become focused on the things that are of God. I call it the Mount of Olive, where you learn about who you are. Then at the Garden of Gethsemane where you can go a little further to carry a conversation with God. Jesus told the disciples about their humanity at the Mount of Olive, near the garden, and then went a little further to pray to the Father in the Garden of Gethsemane. He even led three of the eleven Apostles with Him a bit more in the garden, but He couldn't make them pray, and they were the closest to Him of the twelve: James, Peter, and John. You could lead a horse to water, but you can't make the horse drink it.

If you do not allow the Holy Spirit of God to sanctify you, then you are powerless against the enemy. The Carnal-minded is absent of the knowledge of God and does not understand the renewing of the minds. They constantly need their hands held, as do babies. They are babies in Christ refusing growth unto spiritual maturity. They cannot defend themselves against the wares of Satan. They do not know how yet to submit unto God. They do not yet know how to resist the devil. They are unlearned of the ways of God. They cannot wear the Armor of God because they lack the training. They are easily carried to and fro with false teaching because they do not yet know how to discern what is of God. They find themselves involved in matters they do not wish for because they do not sense or learn how to prove what are the things of God. They don't find themselves living the lifestyle of the lay Christian because they are not equipping their new nature in Christ. 1 John 5:18 (KJV) "We know that whosoever is born of God sinneth not; but he that is begotten of God keepeth himself, and that wicked one toucheth him not." Satan cannot touch the soul of the saved, but he can throw stones at them. Those not in God's word could become confused and waver in their faith.

The worldly and carnal-minded Christians find themselves caught up in fleshly manifestations because they do not know better. They are not mature enough to keep themselves from the clutches of the wicked one, but the Christians have eternal life, so Satan does not touch their souls. God protects the babes in Christ as He protects the Lay-Christian. The Christian can keep himself because he is of God. It's one thing to be caught up in the flesh, and it is another thing to become what you are caught up in, as matters of the flesh.

God chastises His own through the Holy Spirit. To grieve the Holy Spirit is to continue in the opposite way of God when your heart becomes hardened like a stone. God takes away the heart of stone when we are converted and gives us a heart of flesh. He writes His commandments on the table of our fleshly hearts. A fleshly heart is a heart that keeps God's commandments. Those who are of God will occasionally be holy as God is holy, and the reverse for those who are not. Pray that you are of God. Practice the things that are of God and receive the promises of God.

Duties of the Saved

Children of God are to carry their cross daily (Luke 9:23). They are to put themselves under subjection and to examine themselves always to make sure that they are doing the things of God (2 Corinthians 13:5). This is your reasonable service to present yourselves holy and acceptable to the Father (Romans 12:1). Be careful not to preach (all Christians) without putting yourself under subjection (1 Corinthians 9:27) and to not forsake the people of God (Hebrew 10:25).

John 15:2-5 (KJV)

2 Every branch in me that beareth not fruit he taketh away: and every branch that beareth fruit, he purgeth it, that it may bring forth more fruit.

3 Now ye are clean through the word which I have spoken unto you.

4 Abide in me, and I in you. As the branch cannot bear fruit of itself, except it abide in the vine; no more can ye, except ye abide in me.

5 I am the vine, ye are the branches: He that abideth in me, and I in him, the same bringeth forth much fruit: for without me ye can do nothing.

One Kind of Non-Christian: Carnal

The Carnal-minded had become a way to explain a child of God that should be ready to teach God's word, but they refuse to study God's word and remain to be like a babe in Christ needing to be taught the foundation of the Gospel over and over, as the milk of the Gospel. In their life, situations led to unwanted experiences. They remain to be dangerously close to satisfying the flesh and not God. But the essence of the carnal-minded is worldliness.

The truth of carnal-mindedness cannot be spiritual-minded but is always worldly-mindedness. Worldliness is carnal-mindedness.

Romans 8:5-8 (KJV)

5 For they that are after the flesh do mind the things of the flesh; but they that are after the Spirit the things of the Spirit.

6 For to be carnally minded is death; but to be spiritually minded is life and peace.

7 Because the carnal mind is enmity against God: for it is not subject to the law of God, neither indeed can be.

8 So then they that are in the flesh cannot please God.

Two Views

The Spiritual and The Worldly

The Spiritual will receive the gift of God: Eternal Life, to live physically with God, where every day is better than the day before. There are no more sicknesses, death, crying, pain, and suffering in eternal life with the body not made of man but of God. In the flesh, God takes away the heart of stone and gives us a heart of flesh that provides us with a new spirit. But in eternity, we will also have a body after the will of God.

The Worldly will receive the wages of sin: Death, to be eternally separated from God, which is the second death, and to suffer in both Hell and then in the Lake of Fire and Brimstone, where they will have continual death, crying, pain, sicknesses (death is a sickness and Jesus is the cure from it), suffering, dispel, and torment. It is in the Lake of Fire and Brimstone that all authority is lost, where Satan, death, the false prophet, and the sinner are all helpless and beyond hope. God can kill both the body and the soul, but Satan, who blinds the sinner, sends his soul to be destroyed. You should fear Satan, who could lead the soul to destruction, John 10:10. You should fear God, who can kill the soul in hell, Matthew 10:28.

Firstly: Those of the world will choose the lesser powers what to do with radiant thoughts or uncontrollable thoughts that are entering our minds. There is a wrong, a right (sometimes what feels right is misleading, being right does not make it of God), and then a godly. Having a genius thought, ideal, or epiphany does not necessarily mean it is the divine way.

1 John 4:5 (KJV) "They are of the world: therefore speak they of the world, and the world heareth them." In circumstance, situation, or problem, the worldly will not give unto the things of God but unto the things of the world.

Secondly: Those who are of God have a higher power on what to do with radiant thoughts or uncontrollable thoughts entering the mind. Yet, we must tune in to God's voice to hear Him direct us, which could come from circumstances, devotion, prayer, others, or the voice within.

1 John 4:6 (KJV) "We are of God: he that knoweth God heareth us; he that is not of God heareth not us. Hereby know we the spirit of truth, and the spirit of error."

God's Purposes

God made for Himself the Godly and the Ungodly

The Godly

So then, we are called to make the best of the best when making up our minds to do the godly thing. The right thing is not always the best because every man is right in his way, but the sacred thing is always the best. God made man in His image, and in the Garden of Eden, God communicated with Adam. Man of God today is the light of the world and its favor. Christians are the face of God and vessels of God.

Romans 12:1-2 (KJV)

1 I beseech you therefore, brethren, by the mercies of God, that ye present your bodies a living sacrifice, holy, acceptable unto God, which is your reasonable service.

2 And be not conformed to this world: but be ye transformed by the renewing of your mind, that ye may prove what is that good, and acceptable, and perfect, will of God.

The Ungodly

What is right is more suitable for the flesh than one might think. Then how is the right thing the wrong thing?

Proverbs 21:2 (KJV)

2 Every way of a man is right in his own eyes: but the LORD pondereth the hearts.

Proverbs 16:1-5 (KJV)

1 The preparations of the heart in man, and the answer of the tongue, is from the LORD.

2 All the ways of a man are clean in his own eyes; but the LORD weigheth the spirits.

3 Commit thy works unto the LORD, and thy thoughts shall be established.

4 The LORD hath made all things for himself: yea, even the wicked for the day of evil.

5 Every one that is proud in heart is an abomination to the LORD: though hand join in hand, he shall not be unpunished.

To be forsaken by God is beyond what we could imagine. Who knows what that feels like, except Jesus when He took on the world's sins on the cross and was forsaken by the Father because of our sins? Yet Jesus was without sin and worthy to defeat death and hades. And rose on the third day with all power and the keys of life and death in His hands and later ascended on high to be seated at the right hand of the Father. And now we too have victory over death because of Jesus. 2 Corinthians 5:21 (KJV) "For he hath made him to be sin for us, who knew no sin; that we might be made the righteousness of God in him."

CHAPTER SIX

Thy Kingdom Come

1 John 2:1-2 (KJV)

[1] My little children, these things write I unto you, that ye sin not. And if any man sin, we have an advocate with the Father, Jesus Christ the righteous:

[2] And he is the propitiation for our sins: and not for ours only, but also for *the sins of* the whole world.

God loves His whole creation and would have no man perish. And because of this, God's grace and mercy allow us to have heaven on earth. God had promised since the prophets of the Old Testament the promised seed. But the Word of God speaks to those with the Spirit of God because we can only understand by the Holy Spirit. The children of God are aware that we are all sinners, and by the blood of Jesus, the wages of our sins Jesus paid in full. Christ is a propitiation for our sins had allowed all men to resurrect from the grave, but not all men will escape from the unquenchable fire. Christ did not just die for the saved; he died that all men should live with God, but not so.

The way to the heavenly Father is through Jesus Christ. John 3:16 (KJV) "For God so loved the world, that he gave his only begotten Son, that whosoever believeth in him should not perish, but have everlasting life," and Romans 10:9-10 (KJV) "That if thou shalt confess with thy mouth the Lord Jesus, and shalt believe in thine heart that God hath raised him from the dead, thou shalt be saved. For with the heart man believeth unto righteousness; and with the mouth confession is made unto salvation."

All Sins

Jesus is the key to the door of salvation. The key is known to man, but man chooses to remain in darkness. The desires of their flesh outweigh the passion of their souls. It is not God's choice that they remain in ignorance but they do by their own will.

Remember that there are two foundations: Life or death, Jesus or Satan, meaning Of the Blood or Not, Romans 6:23

(KJV) "For the wages of sin is death; but the gift of God is eternal life through Jesus Christ our Lord." There is no in-between.

There are two resurrections: The saved in Christ in the 1st resurrection and the dead in Christ in the 2nd resurrection. The 1st resurrected with Christ in heaven, the place of the Kingdom of God. The 2nd resurrected is judged before the Throne of God to eternal condemnation.

Kingdom of Heaven on Earth: Physically

Matthew 4:16-17 (ASV)

16 the people that sat in darkness saw a great light, and to them that sat in the region and shadow of death, to them did light spring up.

17 From that time began Jesus to preach, and to say, Repent ye; for the kingdom of heaven is at hand.

Jesus was that light during his time on earth, being called a Nazarene that sprung up. Today, the disciples of God, which are all believers that are witnessing that light that springs up, including the five-fold ministry, are all that light that springs up by the indwelling of the Holy Ghost: the concept of that but is not biblical for today is the office of Apostle, and then there are the offices of Prophet, Evangelist, Pastor, and Teacher all functioning in the church today. If we are not shining as the light in the world, then we fail to be salt. If we have nothing to give: a testimony, to witness, to speak of Christ, then we are dead in Christ and are not the light in the world. Those in Christ have a call to the ministry of reconciliation, 2 Corinthians 5:19 (KJV) "To wit, that God was in Christ, reconciling the world unto himself, not imputing their trespasses unto them; and hath committed unto us the word of reconciliation." Even a babe in Christ has a burn to share their testimony.

Let's discuss the five-fold ministry before moving on. The five-fold ministry is biblical in Ephesians 4, the understanding of the ministry of reconciliation.

Ephesians 4: 11-12 (KJV)

[11] And he gave some, apostles; and some, prophets; and some, evangelists; and some, pastors and teachers;

[12] For the perfecting of the saints, for the work of the ministry, for the edifying of the body of Christ:

The only part that separates this from today, but not back then, is the one "Apostle" gift for the 12 Apostles and Paul. Meaning that they physically saw Jesus Christ and were given three tasks: 1) to lay the foundation of the church, 2) to receive, declare, and write God's Word, and 3) to confirm the Word through signs, wonders, and miracles.

Today, we read what is known to us as the Word of God. We call it the Bible. Nobody of our time is qualified to rewrite or co-author the Bible. Paul said he was the least of the apostles and the last to be documented in the New Testament. God's Word does not contradict itself.

Revealed To All: Thy Kingdom Come (Physically on earth)

Jesus Revealed to All

1 John 2:1-2 (ASV)

[1] My little children, these things write I unto you that ye may not sin. And if any man sin, we have an Advocate with the Father, Jesus Christ the righteous:

[2] and he is the propitiation for our sins; and not for ours only, but also for *the whole world.*

God, through His prophets been revealing the savior of the world. Since the Old Testament, God spoke to Abraham about making Him the Father of a great nation. God through the prophet Nathan, David's throne forever established. And all recognized the star from the east that a governor, the shepherd of Israel, is now born. Today, the church (one body (united), many members (people), and one head (Christ)) is the new Israel adopted into the family of Abraham by the blood of Jesus Christ.

Thy Kingdom Come: Physically

Jesus made it apparent that He was the whole package. He is the content of the kingdom of heaven. The joy in heaven is also in the present physical on earth. Even while Jesus performed miracles on earth, He represented the reality of heaven. On earth, as it is in heaven, is offered to those that would receive God's grace. The grace God had promised since man realized the need to repent from sin. Jesus is the gift that gives meaning to God's grace. Jesus is the gift, the promised seed of salvation for all sinners in the world if accepted.

God does not force acceptance of His grace. God offers what is His to be received by choice. Only by accepting God's grace do we experience the attributes of "on earth, as it is in heaven." As Jesus was born into this world by the virgin Mary, God is the kingdom of heaven to come again. Being in Christ is to have a residence in heaven to be with God. King God is the kingdom of heaven because it is in Him that all things exist. Matthew 4:17 (ASV)

"From that time began Jesus to preach, and to say, Repent ye; for the kingdom of heaven is at hand."

To The Lost, To The Carnal Minded Christian, and To The Laity Christian

Isaiah 53:1 (ASV) "Who hath believed our message? and to whom hath the arm of Jehovah been revealed?"

To The Lost

Romans 1:20-21 (KJV)

20 For the invisible things of him from the creation of the world are clearly seen, being understood by the things that are made, *even* his eternal power and Godhead; so that they are without excuse:

21 Because that, when they knew God, they glorified *him* not as God, neither were thankful; but became vain in their imaginations, and their foolish heart was darkened.

God sends a sign to all His creation to see His works. God is invisible to the naked eye, but we see the wonders of His magnificent designs. Satan blinds us from the awesomeness of God through the working of deceit. Satan is the father of all lies. Lies lead to deceitfulness in all aspects.

John 8:44 (KJV) "Ye are of *your* father the devil, and the lusts of your father ye will do. He was a murderer from the beginning, and abode not in the truth, because there is no truth in him. When he speaketh a lie, he speaketh of his own: for he is a liar, and the father of it."

The prophet Isaiah understood that those in darkness would not permanently be blinded. But the unsaved will remain in darkness even though they have seen the light, only because they Will it to themselves. They continue to call deceit their truth and call the world's light to be deceit. You could believe in God and still be in darkness because you have no work. Meaning you walk in disobedience, which is equivalent to disbelief. The ones who heartedly believe are the ones who receive. The ones that repent are the ones following.

John 3:19-20 (ASV)

"And this is the judgment, that the light is come into the world, and men loved the darkness rather than the light; for their works were evil.

For every one that doeth evil hateth the light, and cometh not to the light, lest his works should be reproved."

The Carnal Minded

Hebrews 5:12-13 (KJV)

[12] For when for the time ye ought to be teachers, ye have need that one teach you again which *be* the first principles of the oracles of God; and are become such as have need of milk, and not of strong meat.

[13] For every one that useth milk *is* unskilful in the word of righteousness: for he is a babe.

The carnal-minded are not lost in Christ but are ignorant of the Holy Ghost filling. You have the fullness of the Spirit of God who indwells in you, but you refuse to give your fullness to be empowered by the Spirit of God. You still desire the things of the flesh, but you, like the lost, remain ignorant. But the ignorance of the carnal-minded is not learning of the power that indwells within you. The uplift is that the carnal-minded have faith as big as a mustard seed (believing and confessing Jesus) so they can avoid the fate of the unquenchable fire, but they must give an account of their actions and reactions, as do we all.

Jesus used the parable of the Mustard Seed with the Apostles. Their faith was not yet fully developed, but even in their carnal state, they would have been able to exercise the indwelling powers of the Holy Ghost as they walked with Jesus the Christ (Mark 6:7) and did those that believed before them: Noah, Abraham, Moses, The Judges, David, the prophets all did of God under the inspiration of the Holy Ghost and John the Baptist is the exceptional proof of being filled with the Holy Ghost. The Holy Ghost empowers us all to speak on the things of God. The Apostles received the full development in the Upper Room when the Holy Spirit was sent back to them by Jesus Christ's request to the Father.

The ignorance of the carnal-minded is being mistaken as truth and seeing truth as negativity. When the carnal-minded get something that excites as a benefit, they do not weigh who it is from, its worthiness from God or not. Yet they credit it to God. But God is no longer their focus when they get what they do not want. The carnal-minded remove their eyes from faith and focuses on what is revealed to them by sight.

The ignorance of the Carnal Minded, they spend more time walking by sight than by faith and tend to think their basic understanding has the same honor as those practicing walking by faith. The carnal-minded fail to see what the true significance of faith is.

Romans 12:1-3 (KJV) "I beseech you therefore, brethren, by the mercies of God, that ye present your bodies a living sacrifice, holy, acceptable unto *God*, which is your reasonable service. And be not conformed to this world: but be ye transformed by the renewing of your mind, that ye may prove what is that good, and acceptable, and perfect, will of God. For I say, through the grace given unto me, to every man that is among you, not to think of himself more highly than he ought to think; but to think soberly, according as God hath dealt to every man the measure of faith."

The Laity: The Heavenly Kingdom on Earth: Spiritually

Hebrews 5:14 (KJV) "But strong meat belongeth to them that are of full age, *even* those who by reason of use have their senses exercised to discern both good and evil."

The book of Hebrews makes it known to the believers that the laity in Christ is with spiritual understanding and that they are with the experience of discerning the things of God or not.

The lay Christian understands that Jesus spoke of himself and that the Kingdom of Heaven is at hand. Jesus walked among the people of that time as the kingdom of God. Jesus told them what they needed to do and what He was about to do so they could have heaven on earth.

The Apostle Paul reveals the power of the gospel of Jesus Christ in regards that the inner-man seeks the true nature of God within, no matter who he is, and in 1 John 2:8 (ASV), "Again, a new commandment write I unto you, which thing is true in him and in you; because the darkness is passing away, and the true light already shineth."

The lay Christians understand that today the Heavenly Kingdom resides within them by the indwelling of the Holy Ghost. The inner gift is produced, planted, and inherited because Jesus Christ is the propitiation of our sin being paid for in full. By faith, Christians can believe and understand Matthew 6:10 (KJV) "Thy kingdom come. Thy will be done in earth, as *it is* in heaven."

Christians are privileged as the children of God: we are not of the world but are in the world with God's blessings upon us. We are God's Kingdom on earth, and because of God's promise to Abraham, even David, the Holy Ghost indwells in us. We should recognize all men as the earth in this regard and not the world, yet man originates from land. We in Christ give population to the physical Heavenly Kingdom, which is also in us spiritually. We are created from the dust of the earth by God's hands. Ashes to Ashes and dust to dust. God is the author, the potter; God's will is carried out to save. Jesus made it possible for God to take pleasure in us. So, God's heavenly kingdom is within us. Because of His son's blood, God can chastise, settle, and establish us in Him.

John 14:23 (KJV)

23 Jesus answered and said unto him, If a man love me, he will keep my words: and my Father will love him, and we will come unto him, and make our abode with him.

Galatians 2:20 (KJV)

20 I am crucified with Christ: nevertheless I live; yet not I, but Christ liveth in me: and the life which I now live in the flesh I live by the faith of the Son of God, who loved me, and gave himself for me.

Colossians 1:27 (KJV)

27 To whom God would make known what *is* the riches of the glory of this mystery among the Gentiles; which is Christ in you, the hope of glory:

Kingdom Come Literally

Two Instances: The Millennium Kingdom of Jesus Christ and God appearing on His Throne at Judgement and Newness.

The actual placement of Thy Kingdom Come with Jesus. The period of Jesus Christ's Kingdom on earth and to follow is God's heavenly kingdom to come before the new heaven and earth.

Second Coming/Millennium 1000-Year Reign with Jesus

The first resurrection in Christ, they belong to God. They excepted the Son of God, the Son of Man, as their Lord and Savior. They claim the blood of Jesus to be sufficient in paying the price for their sins. They will have the gift of God, which is eternal life, having a crown of life and jewels of the establishment. They of the second resurrection will not have power towards life but will suffer eternal death. Eternal death is being separated from the Father forever. To be forever without hope of deliverance from the lake that burns with fire and brimstone.

Revelation 20:4-6 (KJV)

[4] And I saw thrones, and they sat upon them, and judgment was given unto them: and *I saw* the souls of them that were beheaded for the witness of Jesus, and for the word of God, and which had not worshipped the beast, neither his image, neither had received *his* mark upon their foreheads, or in their hands; and they lived and reigned with Christ a thousand years. [5] But the rest of the dead lived not again until the thousand years were finished. This *is* the first resurrection.

[6] Blessed and holy *is* he that hath part in the first resurrection: on such the second death hath no power, but they shall be priests of God and of Christ, and shall reign with him a thousand years.

The Coming of the Lord Suddenly

The seven-year Tribulation ends with Jesus putting His foot down, representing His second coming that starts the Millennium. Jesus will send His angels with a great sound of a trumpet to gather His people together for the Millennium. Jesus will establish His physical Kingdom on Earth, and those in Christ will be the residents of its royal nation; Zechariah 14:3-4 (KJV)

"Then shall the LORD go forth, and fight against those nations, as when he fought in the day of battle.

And his feet shall stand in that day upon the mount of Olives, which *is* before Jerusalem on the east, and the mount of Olives shall cleave in the midst thereof toward the east and toward the west, *and there shall be* a very great valley; and half of the mountain shall remove toward the north, and half of it toward the south." God shall elevate Jerusalem above its surroundings. He shall flatten the surroundings of Jerusalem.

Examination Time

1 Corinthians 15:25, 27(ASV) "For he must reign, till he hath put all his enemies under his feet. For, He put all things in subjection under his feet. But when he saith, All things are put in subjection, it is evident that he is excepted who did subject all things unto him."

- Jesus will revenge the church body, who are the saved in Christ.
- Then the people of the world who say that God does not care shall see the coming of the Lord, and then the people who say that God does not intervene will see the appearance of the Lord.
- They will see the eradication of evil because Jesus' Kingdom shall subdue the world for righteousness' sake, and there will be peace for one thousand years.
- The enemy of God shall flee, and the children of God come to the Holy Land of Jerusalem, where God shall establish the Kingdom of the Lord. It will become one day for the Lord, 1000 years with us.

Jesus' glory will light the world, and the whole world will partake of it.

Zechariah 14:5-7 (KJV)

[5] And ye shall flee *to* the valley of the mountains; for the valley of the mountains shall reach unto Azal: yea, ye shall flee, like as ye fled from before the earthquake in the days of Uzziah king of Judah: and the LORD my God shall come, *and* all the saints with thee.

[6] And it shall come to pass in that day, *that* the light shall not be clear, *nor* dark:

[7] But it shall be one day which shall be known to the LORD, not day, nor night: but it shall come to pass, *that* at evening time it shall be light.

- Living Waters and Peace
- These living waters will be healing power to the children of God.
- Remember that even the Jews that witnessed the two witnesses at the gate murdered on the third day rose again, and when God called to them, the two witnesses ascended, those Jews they had all repented.
- The knowing in partial the gospel of Jesus Christ shall be no more partisan; every mouth shall confess, and every knee shall bow to Jesus as the one and only Lord.

There will be true peace in the land of the Children of God for one thousand years and end at the War of Armageddon.

- God will then physically protect the Saints by raining fire and brimstone on the enemy before the enemy could touch Jerusalem, where his children are. Today God saves us spiritually and physically by intervening on our behalf according to His purpose.

Zechariah 14:8-11 (KJV)

[8] And it shall be in that day, *that* living waters shall go out from Jerusalem; half of them toward the former sea, and half of them toward the hinder sea: in summer and in winter shall it be.

[9] And the LORD shall be king over all the earth: in that day shall there be one LORD, and his name one.

¹⁰ All the land shall be turned as a plain from Geba to Rimmon south of Jerusalem: and it shall be lifted up, and inhabited in her place, from Benjamin's gate unto the place of the first gate, unto the corner gate, and *from* the tower of Hananeel unto the king's winepresses.

¹¹ And *men* shall dwell in it, and there shall be no more utter destruction; but Jerusalem shall be safely inhabited.

¹² And this shall be the plague wherewith the LORD will smite all the people that have fought against Jerusalem; Their flesh shall consume away while they stand upon their feet, and their eyes shall consume away in their holes, and their tongue shall consume away in their mouth.

¹³ And it shall come to pass in that day, *that* a great tumult from the LORD shall be among them; and they shall lay hold every one on the hand of his neighbour, and his hand shall rise up against the hand of his neighbour.

¹⁴ And Judah also shall fight at Jerusalem; and the wealth of all the heathen round about shall be gathered together, gold, and silver, and apparel, in great abundance.

¹⁵ And so shall be the plague of the horse, of the mule, of the camel, and of the ass, and of all the beasts that shall be in these tents, as this plague.

- God will plague those against Him and keep the rain from them. They will suffer from famine, drought, pain, blindness, and sicknesses by plaque.
- The people, excluding God's enemies, will come doing the Feast of Tabernacle: A Festival of Thanksgiving to celebrate the harvest of the human souls. Jesus Christ died on the cross and initiated The Feast of Passover: The Day of Atonement. The Feast of First Fruit at Christ's resurrection and the coming of the Holy Spirit at Pentecost.
- The people of God shall have refuge in Jerusalem doing these times.
- This plague points to the speaking in two instances. Firstly, in the past, God's wrath was a punishment for the disobedience of Israel doing the time of Zechariah. Secondly, that is still to come in the future for the disobedient. Those who refuse to reverence the Lord will not honor the Feast of the Tabernacle.
- Still, God will subdue and bring all things in subjection unto Himself,

Zechariah 14:16-19 (KJV)

[16] And it shall come to pass, *that* every one that is left of all the nations which came against Jerusalem shall even go up from year to year to worship the King, the LORD of hosts, and to keep the feast of tabernacles.

[17] And it shall be, *that* whoso will not come up of *all* the families of the earth unto Jerusalem to worship the King, the LORD of hosts, even upon them shall be no rain.

[18] And if the family of Egypt go not up, and come not, that *have* no *rain*; there shall be the plague, wherewith the LORD will smite the heathen that come not up to keep the feast of tabernacles.

[19] This shall be the punishment of Egypt, and the punishment of all nations that come not up to keep the feast of tabernacles.

Holy Jerusalem

- Everything in Jerusalem will be holy consecrated for sacrifices for the Feast of Tabernacle, which is the only feast today not fulfilled. God shall rid His kingdom of evil.
- The evil shall not have a part in the realm of Jesus Christ for the duration of the Millennium. Those that choose to give honor to the Feast of the
- The Tabernacle shall partake in the holiness of Jerusalem. In the end, the Lord of Host proves Himself as the Son of God. The Savoir, Lamb of God, the Vine, the perfect penitent for sin. Jesus rules His kingdom on earth for 1000 years (Matthew 24:27-31; Revelation 20: 4-6).

Zechariah 14:20-21 (KJV)

[20] In that day shall there be upon the bells of the horses, HOLINESS UNTO THE LORD; and the pots in the LORD'S house shall be like the bowls before the altar.

21 Yea, every pot in Jerusalem and in Judah shall be holiness unto the LORD of hosts: and all they that sacrifice shall come and take of them, and seethe therein: and in that day there shall be no more the Canaanite in the house of the LORD of hosts.

God Appears on His Throne on Earth

The day of judgment is the day God shall show His face. The Saints in the Lord shall share in judging even the angles with God, 1 Corinthians 6:3.

On the Day of Judgment, the deserving shall have God's final mercies; for example: what about the Egyptian mother who cared for Moses? Matthew 25:40 (KJV) "And the King shall answer and say unto them, Verily I say unto you, Inasmuch as ye have done it unto one of the least of these my brethren, ye have done it unto me."t

God will redeem/reward some standing before Him, but He will not save the souls of those dead in Christ. Satan would not have deceived all flesh to wage war against the Saints in Jerusalem.

Revelation 20:11-15 (KJV)

11 And I saw a great white throne, and him that sat on it, from whose face the earth and the heaven fled away; and there was found no place for them.

12 And I saw the dead, small and great, stand before God; and the books were opened: and another book was opened, which is *the book* of life: and the dead were judged out of those things which were written in the books, according to their works.

13 And the sea gave up the dead which were in it; and death and hell delivered up the dead which were in them: and they were judged every man according to their works.

14 And death and hell were cast into the lake of fire. This is the second death.

15 And whosoever was not found written in the book of life was cast into the lake of fire.

- New Heaven and Earth and the City of Jerusalem
- The new heaven and earth shall not come before the judgment of the wicked.
- The lost souls not in God will not witness this moment. Only the bride of God will have the joy of this new event from God. The saved in Christ lives forever in the presence of God, the creator of everything that had and will exist.

Revelation 21:1-8 (KJV)

[1] "And I saw a new heaven and a new earth: for the first heaven and the first earth were passed away; and there was no more sea.

[2] And I John saw the holy city, new Jerusalem, coming down from God out of heaven, prepared as a bride adorned for her husband.

[3] And I heard a great voice out of heaven saying, Behold, the tabernacle of God *is* with men, and he will dwell with them, and they shall be his people, and God himself shall be with them, *and be* their God.

[4] And God shall wipe away all tears from their eyes; and there shall be no more death, neither sorrow, nor crying, neither shall there be any more pain: for the former things are passed away.

[5] And he that sat upon the throne said, Behold, I make all things new. And he said unto me, Write: for these words are true and faithful."

- The eternal promises of God are summed up as Alpha and Omega, the beginning and the end. God is outside of time as we would know it to be. Time does not exist to God, for God always existed. An eternity with God is not enough to know everything about God. An eternity with God is forever, and eternity cannot define God.

[6] "And he said unto me, It is done. I am Alpha and Omega, the beginning and the end. I will give unto him that is athirst of the fountain of the water of life freely.

[7] He that overcometh shall inherit all things; and I will be his God, and he shall be my son.

[8] But the fearful, and unbelieving, and the abominable, and murderers, and whoremongers, and sorcerers, and idolaters, and all liars, shall have their part in the lake which burneth with fire and brimstone: which is the second death."

Printed in the United States
by Baker & Taylor Publisher Services